The AI-Driven Lawyer

Adapting to Artificial Intelligence in the Legal Profession

CHIRAG KANSARA

Made with ❤️ on the Notion Press Platform

To all the dedicated legal professionals worldwide,

This book is for you—the steadfast advocates of justice, the guardians of the rule of law, and the diligent practitioners who navigate the complexities of the legal landscape with integrity and perseverance. Your unwavering commitment to upholding ethical standards and delivering exceptional service inspires us daily. May this book serve as a guide and a beacon as you embrace the transformative power of Artificial Intelligence, helping you enhance your invaluable work and lead your practice into a bright, innovative future.

With gratitude and admiration,

Chirag Kansara

Contents

FOREWORD: VII
PROLOGUE/INTRODUCTION IX
INTRODUCTION TO ARTIFICIAL INTELLIGENCE IN THE LEGAL PROFESSION 13
PRIVACY AND DATA SECURITY CONCERNS 25
ETHICAL IMPLICATIONS OF AI IN LEGAL PRACTICE 31
BUILDING A LEGAL AI FRAMEWORK FOR LAW FIRMS 37
TRAINING AND DEVELOPMENT FOR AI INTEGRATION 43
ADAPTING LAW FIRM BUSINESS MODELS IN THE AGE OF AI 49
NAVIGATING ETHICAL AND REGULATORY CHALLENGES IN AI ADOPTION55
ADDRESSING PRIVACY AND SECURITY CONCERNS IN AI ADOPTION 61
EVALUATING AND SELECTING AI VENDORS FOR LEGAL PRACTICE 67
EMERGING TRENDS AND NOTABLE STARTUPS IN LEGAL AI 73
INDIAN LEGAL AI STARTUPS TRANSFORMING THE LEGAL LANDSCAPE 79
TOP 25 AI TOOLS REVOLUTIONIZING LEGAL PRACTICE 85
TOP 25 AI TOOLS REVOLUTIONIZING LEGAL PRACTICE 87
IMPLEMENTING AI IN LEGAL WORKFLOWS: A STEP-BY-STEP GUIDE FOR LAW FIRMS 91
IMPLEMENTING AI IN LEGAL WORKFLOWS: A STEP-BY-STEP GUIDE FOR LAW FIRMS 93

Foreword:

The dawn of Artificial Intelligence (AI) has brought transformative changes across all sectors, and the legal profession is no exception. As the world stands at the brink of a new era where technology and human expertise intersect, it becomes imperative to explore how AI can redefine law practice—enhancing efficiency, improving accuracy, and reshaping how legal services are delivered.

This book, **"The AI-Driven Lawyer: Adapting to Artificial Intelligence in the Legal Profession,"** arrives at a critical moment. It comprehensively examines AI's potential to transform legal practice, from streamlining case research and automating document review to predictive analytics forecasting case outcomes. Yet, this transformation goes beyond technology; it dives into ethical considerations and the importance of responsible AI usage, a crucial element in maintaining trust and ensuring fair legal practices.

As a technology professional with years of experience, I've witnessed firsthand the profound impact of technological advancements—the balance of opportunities and challenges AI brings to the legal field. This book is designed not merely as a theoretical exploration but as a practical guide grounded in real-world applications, making it an invaluable resource for lawyers at all levels.

The chapters outline a step-by-step roadmap, guiding legal practitioners from understanding the foundational AI use cases to navigating implementation complexities and measuring their impact. The emphasis is on starting small, learning continuously, and scaling strategically. Each chapter builds on the previous one, providing a manageable and impactful view of integrating AI into legal workflows.

This book guides law professionals seeking to harness AI's transformative power while adhering to core values of justice, transparency, and ethical practice. The future of law is not about replacing lawyers with machines but about augmenting human expertise with intelligent systems, unlocking new potentials in the pursuit of justice.

As you embark on this journey of discovery and innovation, may you find inspiration, practical guidance, and a renewed sense of purpose. The path ahead is filled with opportunities, and with the right approach, we can create a legal profession that is efficient, innovative, fair and inclusive.

Welcome to the future of legal practice.

Sincerely,
Chirag Kansara

Prologue/Introduction

Imagine a legal practice where technology seamlessly supports and enhances every facet of human expertise. A setting where routine tasks are automated, enabling legal professionals to concentrate on strategic initiatives and personal client interactions that drive success. In this envisioned future, Artificial Intelligence (AI) is not merely a tool but a trusted partner, unlocking new efficiency, accuracy, and innovation levels.

This book is your guide into that future.

Traditionally, the legal profession has been rooted in meticulous research, extensive documentation, and adherence to established procedures. Over time, the role of legal practitioners has evolved to encompass strategic advisory, advocacy, and leadership within the justice system. Today, we stand on the brink of another significant transformation driven by AI.

AI promises to revolutionise legal practice in ways we are just beginning to comprehend. It has the potential to streamline legal research, automate document review, predict case outcomes, and much more. However, with great power comes great responsibility. As we integrate AI into legal processes, we must remain vigilant about ethical considerations, data privacy, and the necessity for human oversight.

This book aims to bridge the gap between AI's potential and its practical application in the legal field. It offers a comprehensive guide to navigating this new landscape, providing insights, strategies, and best practices for leveraging AI to enhance rather than replace human capabilities.

Each chapter builds upon the previous one, guiding you through the complexities of AI integration—from identifying initial use cases to scaling AI across your practice. We explore ethical implications, discuss regulatory frameworks, and offer practical steps for ensuring continuous improvement and alignment with professional standards.

You will find a blend of visionary thinking and practical advice as you read through these pages. The future of legal practice is not about choosing between technology and people; it's about finding the right balance that allows both to thrive. By embracing AI thoughtfully and responsibly, we can create more efficient and human-centred legal services.

Welcome to a journey of discovery, innovation, and transformation. The future of the legal profession is here, filled with exciting possibilities.

Let's explore them together.

Chirag Kansara

The AI-Driven Lawyer

Adapting to Artificial Intelligence in the Legal Profession

Introduction to Artificial Intelligence in the Legal Profession

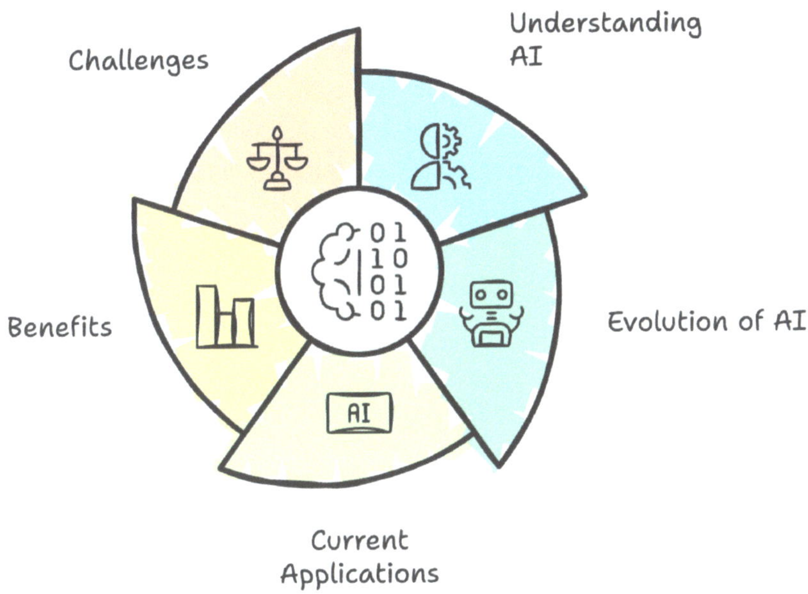

Introduction to Artificial Intelligence in the Legal Profession

1.1 Understanding Artificial Intelligence

Artificial Intelligence (AI) is the simulation of human intelligence processes by machines, particularly computer systems. These processes include learning (acquiring information and rules for using the information), reasoning (using rules to reach approximate or definite conclusions), and self-correction. In the legal context, AI encompasses technologies that can perform legal research, document analysis, and predictive analytics, which traditionally require human intelligence.

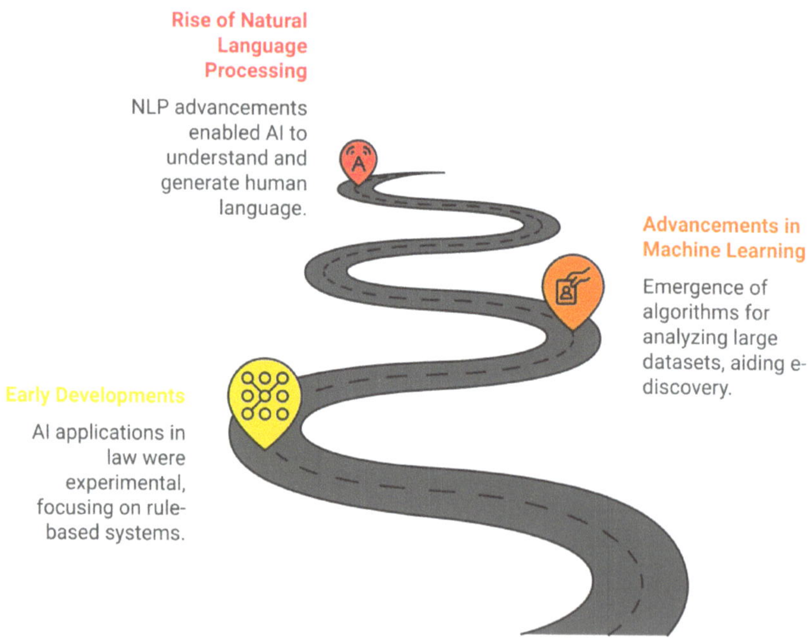

1.2 Evolution of AI in Legal Practice

The integration of AI into legal practice has evolved over several decades:

- **Early Developments:** In the 1980s and 1990s, AI applications in law were primarily experimental, focusing on rule-based systems to assist with legal reasoning and decision-making.
- **Advancements in Machine Learning:** The 2000s saw the emergence of machine learning algorithms capable of analysing large datasets, leading to the development of tools for e-discovery and legal research.
- **Rise of Natural Language Processing (NLP):** Recent advancements in NLP have enabled AI systems to understand and generate human language, facilitating more sophisticated applications such as contract analysis and legal drafting.

1.3 Current Applications of AI in the Legal Sector

AI technologies are currently employed in various aspects of legal practice:

- **Legal Research:** AI-powered platforms can quickly analyse vast legal databases to identify relevant case law, statutes, and regulations, enhancing the efficiency and accuracy of legal research.
- **Document Review and Analysis:** AI tools assist in reviewing and analysing legal documents, identifying pertinent information, and flagging potential issues, which is particularly beneficial in due diligence and discovery processes.
- **Contract Management:** AI systems streamline contract drafting, review, and management by automating repetitive tasks and ensuring compliance with legal standards.

- **Predictive Analytics:** AI can analyse historical case data to predict legal outcomes, aiding lawyers in developing case strategies and risk assessments.

1.4 Benefits of AI Integration in Legal Practice

The incorporation of AI into legal practice offers several advantages:

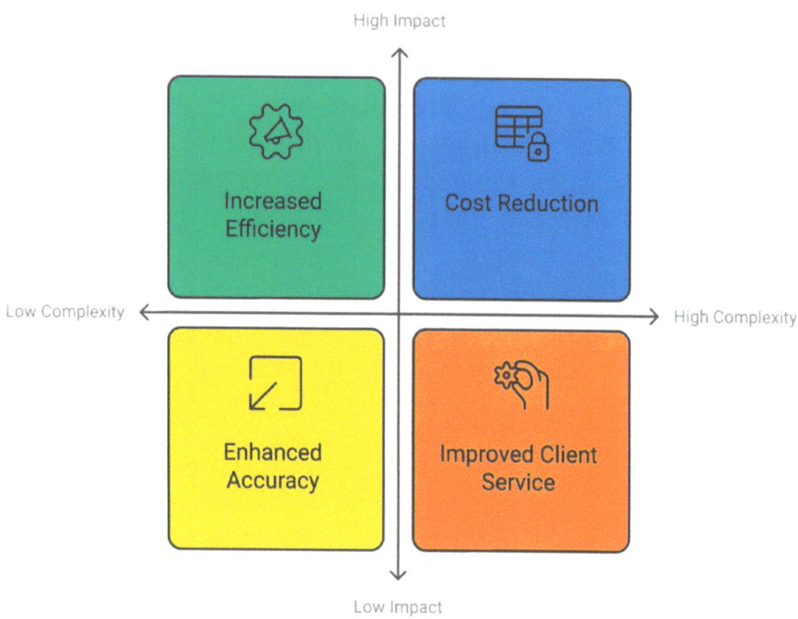

- **Increased Efficiency:** Automation of routine tasks allows legal professionals to focus on more complex and strategic work, improving overall productivity.
- **Cost Reduction:** By streamlining processes, AI can reduce operational costs for law firms and clients.
- **Enhanced Accuracy:** AI systems minimise human errors in tasks such as document review and data analysis, leading to more reliable outcomes.

- **Improved Client Service:** Faster turnaround times and more accurate information enhance client satisfaction and trust.

1.5 Challenges and Considerations

Despite its benefits, AI integration in legal practice presents specific challenges:

- **Ethical Concerns:** Issues related to bias in AI algorithms, transparency, and accountability must be addressed to maintain ethical standards.
- **Data Privacy and Security:** Handling sensitive client information requires robust data protection measures to prevent breaches and comply with regulations.
- **Skill Development:** Legal professionals must acquire new skills to effectively utilise AI tools and interpret their outputs.
- **Regulatory Compliance:** Ensuring that AI applications comply with existing laws and regulations is essential to avoid legal complications.

Understanding these aspects is crucial for legal professionals and firms aiming to integrate AI into their practice responsibly and effectively.

References:

- "Artificial Intelligence in Legal Practice," DRI, (dri.org)
- "AI and the Legal Profession," American Bar Association, (americanbar.org)
- "The Future of Professionals: How AI is impacting the legal profession," Thomson Reuters, (legal.thomsonreuters.com)
- "Generative AI in the Legal Profession," Harvard Law School Center on the Legal Profession, (clp.law.harvard.edu

Enhancing Efficiency, Accuracy, and Client Service

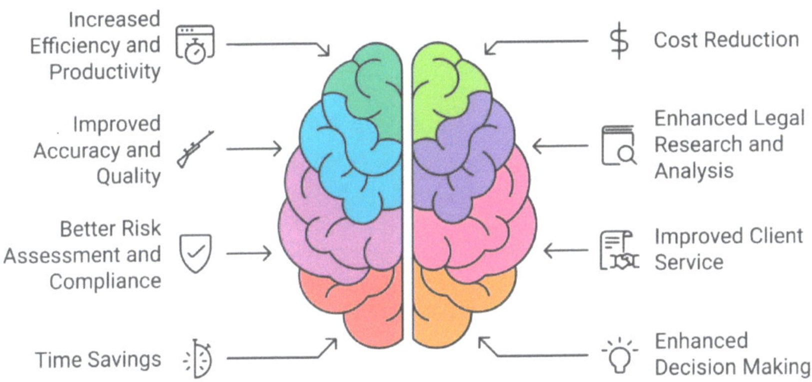

Enhancing Efficiency, Accuracy, and Client Service

Artificial Intelligence (AI) is transforming the legal industry, offering numerous benefits to law firms and legal processes. Here are the key advantages of implementing AI in legal practices:

2.1 Increased Efficiency and Productivity

AI enhances efficiency in legal processes by automating routine tasks such as document review, contract analysis, and legal research. This automation streamlines workflows, reducing time spent on mundane activities and allowing lawyers to focus on higher-value, strategic work.

2.2 Cost Reduction

Implementing AI leads to cost savings by reducing the time spent on labour-intensive tasks and minimising human errors, which can be costly to rectify. Additionally, AI enables law firms to handle more work without increasing staff.

2.3 Improved Accuracy and Quality

AI enhances the quality of legal work by analysing vast amounts of data with high precision, reducing human errors in document review and contract analysis, and providing consistent results across similar tasks.

2.4 Enhanced Legal Research and Analysis

AI-powered tools improve legal research by quickly sifting through extensive legal databases, identifying relevant precedents and case law more efficiently, and offering predictive analytics for case outcomes.

2.5 Better Risk Assessment and Compliance

AI assists in managing legal risks by identifying potential issues in contracts and legal documents, enhancing due diligence processes, and ensuring compliance with changing regulations.

2.6 Improved Client Service

AI enables law firms to provide better client service through faster response times, more accurate information, increased transparency in billing and legal processes, and more cost-effective legal services.

2.7 Time Savings

AI significantly reduces the time spent on document review, e-discovery, contract lifecycle management, legal research, and case analysis.

2.8 Enhanced Decision Making

AI supports legal professionals in making informed decisions by providing data-driven insights, offering predictive analytics for case strategies, and assisting in early risk assessment.

2.9 Competitive Advantage

Law firms adopting AI gain a competitive edge by offering more efficient and cost-effective services, attracting tech-savvy clients, and staying ahead of industry trends and innovations.

By leveraging AI, law firms can transform their operations, improve service delivery, and adapt to the changing landscape of the legal industry. While AI will not replace lawyers, it serves as a powerful tool to augment their capabilities and drive innovation in legal practices

References

- **AI in the Legal Industry**: This article discusses how AI is boosting legal team productivity and outlines the benefits and potential risks of deploying large language models (LLMs) in law practice.

Gartner

- **A Year in Review: How AI Transformed the Legal Profession in 2023**: This piece provides an overview of AI's impact on the legal profession, highlighting key developments and transformations that occurred in 2023.

Thomson Reuters Legal

- **How Is AI Changing the Legal Profession?**: This article explores the ways AI is altering the legal field, including the automation of routine tasks and the challenges associated with AI integration.

Bloomberg Law

- **7 Benefits of AI in the Legal Industry**: This blog post outlines seven key advantages of AI implementation in legal practices, such as increased efficiency, cost reduction, and improved client service.

ContractPodAi

Privacy and Data Security Concerns

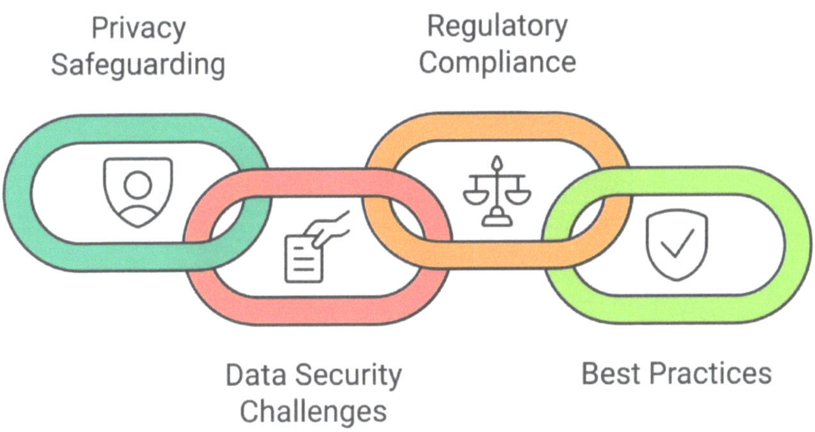

Privacy and Data Security Concerns

3.1 Understanding Privacy in the Context of Legal Tech

Privacy pertains to safeguarding client information and ensuring that sensitive data remains confidential in the legal profession. Integrating Legal Technology introduces complexities in maintaining this confidentiality as digital platforms and cloud-based services become integral to legal operations. Lawyers must ensure technology adoption does not compromise their clients' privacy rights.

3.2 Data Security Challenges in AI and Cloud-Based Legal Solutions

The utilisation of AI and cloud-based solutions in legal practice presents several data security challenges:

- **Data Breaches:** Unauthorized access to digital systems can lead to the exposure of confidential client information.
- **Data Storage and Transmission:** Storing and transmitting data over the Internet increases the risk of interception and unauthorised access.
- **Third-Party Vendors:** Relying on external service providers for data storage and processing necessitates thorough due diligence to ensure they adhere to stringent security protocols.
- **Compliance with Data Protection Laws:** Law firms must navigate complex regulatory landscapes to ensure compliance with data protection laws, which can vary across jurisdictions.

3.3 Regulatory Compliance: GDPR, CCPA, and Other Data Protection Laws

Law firms must comply with various data protection regulations to safeguard client information:

- **General Data Protection Regulation (GDPR):** This regulation applies to entities processing personal data of individuals within the European Union. It mandates strict data protection measures and grants individuals rights over personal data.
- **California Consumer Privacy Act (CCPA):** This U.S. state law provides California residents with rights regarding their personal information, including the right to know what data is collected and the right to request deletion.
- **Other Jurisdictional Laws:** Various countries and states have enacted data protection laws, each with specific requirements that law firms must adhere to when handling client data.

Non-compliance with these regulations can result in significant legal and financial repercussions, including fines and damage to the firm's reputation.

3.4 Best Practices for Data Protection in Legal Tech Adoption

To mitigate privacy and data security risks associated with Legal Tech, law firms should implement the following best practices:

- **Conduct Thorough Due Diligence:** Evaluate technology vendors' security measures and compliance status before adoption.
- **Implement Robust Access Controls:** Ensure only authorised personnel can access sensitive client information.

- **Encrypt Data:** Utilize robust encryption methods for data at rest and in transit to protect against unauthorised access.
- **Regular Security Audits:** Conduct periodic security protocols and systems assessments to identify and address vulnerabilities.
- **Employee Training:** Educate staff on data protection policies, potential threats, and client confidentiality.
- **Develop Incident Response Plans:** Establish clear procedures for responding to data breaches or security incidents to minimise impact and ensure compliance with legal obligations.

By adhering to these practices, law firms can enhance their data protection strategies, ensuring that the integration of Legal Tech does not compromise client privacy and complies with applicable data protection laws.

Ethical Implications of AI in Legal Practice

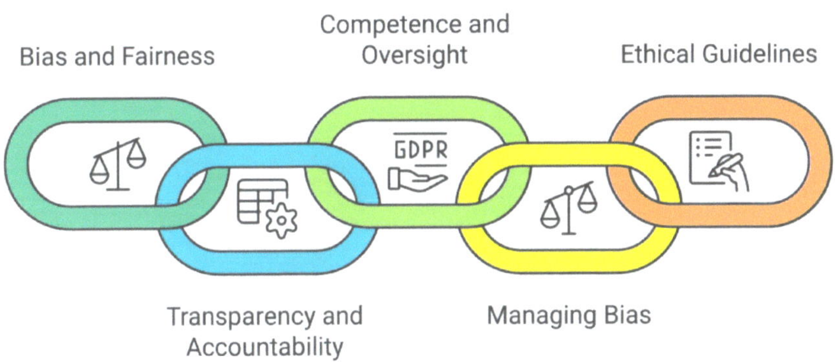

Ethical Implications of AI in Legal Practice

4.1 Overview of Ethical Challenges with AI in Law

The integration of Artificial Intelligence (AI) into legal practice introduces several ethical challenges that legal professionals must navigate:

- **Bias and Fairness:** AI systems can inadvertently perpetuate existing biases in their training data, leading to unfair outcomes in legal contexts. For instance, if an AI tool is trained on historical legal decisions that contain biases, it may continue to reflect those biases in its analyses or recommendations.
- **Transparency and Accountability:** The "black box" nature of some AI algorithms makes it difficult to understand decisions, posing challenges for accountability and transparency in legal processes. This opacity can hinder a lawyer's ability to explain or justify AI-driven decisions to clients or courts.
- **Competence and Oversight:** Lawyers have an ethical duty to provide competent representation, including understanding their tools. Incorporating AI requires lawyers to attain sufficient knowledge to oversee AI applications effectively and ensure they are used appropriately.

4.2 Managing Bias in AI Algorithms and Predictive Analytics

To address and mitigate bias in AI systems, legal professionals should:

- **Assess Training Data:** Evaluate the datasets used to train AI tools to identify and rectify potential biases. Ensuring diverse and representative data can help reduce the risk of biased outcomes.
- **Implement Fairness Audits:** Conduct regular audits of AI systems to detect and address biases. These audits can involve testing the AI's outputs for discriminatory patterns.
- **Engage in Continuous Monitoring:** Regularly monitor AI systems to ensure they operate as intended and not develop or perpetuate biases over time. Continuous oversight allows for timely interventions when issues arise.

4.3 Ensuring Transparency and Fairness in AI Decisions

To promote transparency and fairness in AI-driven legal processes, consider the following practices:

- **Explainability:** Choose AI tools that clearly explain their decisions, enabling lawyers to understand and communicate the rationale behind AI-generated outcomes. This transparency is crucial for maintaining trust and accountability.
- **Human Oversight:** Humans should remain involved in AI-driven processes to review and validate AI outputs. This will ensure that decisions align with ethical standards and legal principles. Human oversight also safeguards against potential errors or biases in AI systems.
- **Develop Ethical Guidelines:** Establish and adhere to ethical guidelines for AI use within the firm, outlining acceptable practices and procedures for addressing ethical dilemmas. These guidelines should be regularly reviewed and updated to reflect evolving standards and technologies.

4.4 Creating Ethical Guidelines for AI Use in Law Firms

Law firms should develop comprehensive ethical guidelines for AI integration, encompassing:

- **Competence:** Ensure that all legal professionals using AI possess adequate knowledge and training to utilise these tools effectively and responsibly. This includes understanding AI systems' capabilities and limitations.
- **Confidentiality:** Implement measures to protect client confidentiality when using AI tools, such as securing data and ensuring that AI providers comply with privacy standards. This is essential to maintain client trust and comply with legal obligations.
- **Informed Consent:** Communicate with clients about using AI in their cases, obtain informed consent and address any concerns they may have about AI involvement. Transparency with clients fosters trust and ensures they know how their information is being handled.
- **Accountability:** Establish clear protocols for accountability, ensuring that legal professionals remain responsible for AI-assisted decisions and actions. This includes setting procedures for addressing errors or issues arising from AI use.

By proactively addressing these ethical considerations, law firms can integrate AI technologies that uphold the integrity of the legal profession and enhance the quality of legal services provided to clients.

Building a Legal AI Framework for Law Firms

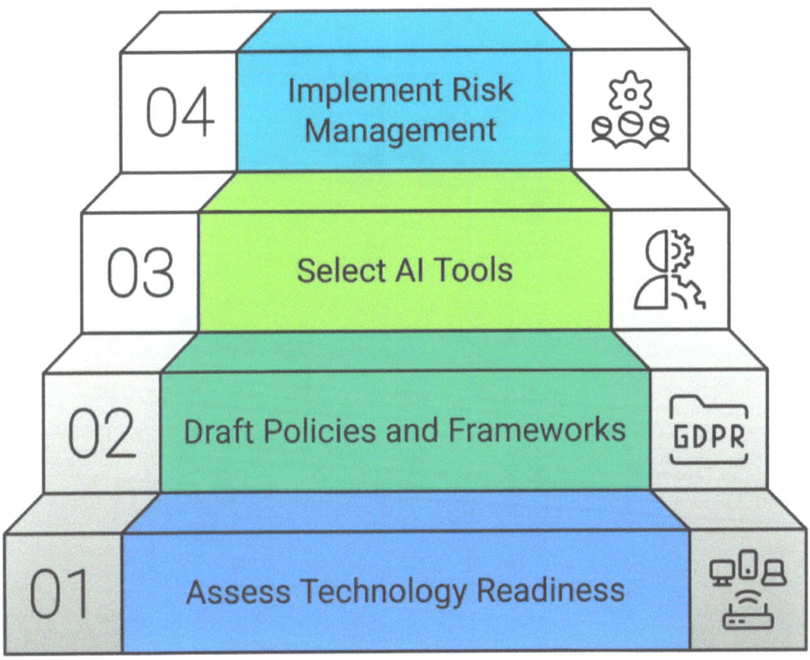

Building a Legal AI Framework for Law Firms

5.1 Assessing Technology Readiness

Before integrating AI into legal practice, law firms should evaluate their technological preparedness:

- **Infrastructure Evaluation:** Assess current IT systems to ensure they can support AI applications, focusing on data storage, processing capabilities, and network security.
- **Staff Competency:** Assess the technological proficiency of legal and support staff and identify areas where training is necessary to use AI tools effectively.
- **Data Management Practices:** Review data collection, storage, and management protocols to ensure data quality and accessibility for AI applications.

5.2 Drafting Policies and Frameworks for AI Integration

Establishing clear policies is crucial for the responsible adoption of AI:

- **Ethical Guidelines:** Develop protocols addressing ethical considerations, such as bias mitigation, transparency, and accountability in AI usage.
- **Data Privacy and Security Policies:** Implement measures to protect client confidentiality and comply with data protection regulations when using AI tools.
- **Usage Policies:** Define acceptable AI applications within the firm, specifying tasks suitable for AI assistance and those requiring human oversight.

5.3 Guidelines for Selecting and Implementing Legal AI Tools

When choosing AI tools, consider the following:

- **Vendor Due Diligence:** Evaluate AI vendors based on their reputation, compliance with legal standards, and commitment to data security.
- **Customisation and Scalability:** Select AI solutions tailored to the firm's needs and scale with growth.
- **User-Friendliness:** Ensure the AI tools are intuitive, facilitating smooth integration into existing workflows without extensive retraining.
- **Support and Maintenance:** To keep the AI tools effective and secure, choose vendors that offer robust support and regular updates.

5.4 Legal AI Risk Management and Mitigation Strategies

To manage risks associated with AI adoption:

- **Regular Audits:** Conduct periodic assessments of AI systems to identify and address potential biases, inaccuracies, or security vulnerabilities.
- **Human Oversight:** Humans should remain involved in AI-assisted tasks to review outputs and make final decisions, ensuring ethical and accurate outcomes.
- **Continuous Training:** To keep pace with technological advancements and educate staff on AI developments, ethical considerations, and best practices.
- **Incident Response Planning:** Develop protocols for responding to AI-related issues, such as data breaches or system errors, to minimise impact and maintain client trust.

By systematically assessing readiness, establishing comprehensive policies, carefully selecting AI tools, and implementing robust risk management strategies, law firms can effectively integrate AI into their practices, enhancing efficiency while upholding ethical and professional standards.

References:

- "Implementing AI Solutions in Law Firms: Best Practices and Challenges," Legal Tech Munch,
- "AI Implementation in Law Firms: 5 Essential Best Practices," Tucan.ai
- "Risk Management for Legal AI Solutions," Kelvin. legal,
- "A Roadmap for Integrating AI at Your Law Firm," Centerbase

Training and Development for AI Integration

Training and Development for AI Integration

6.1 Importance of Training Legal Professionals in AI

Integrating Artificial Intelligence (AI) into legal practice requires legal professionals to acquire a foundational understanding of AI technologies. This knowledge enables them to effectively use AI tools, ensuring that these technologies enhance rather than hinder their practice. Moreover, informed legal professionals can better address ethical considerations and maintain the quality of client services.

6.2 Identifying Key Skills and Competencies

To effectively integrate AI into legal workflows, legal professionals should develop the following skills:

- **Technical Literacy:** A basic understanding of AI concepts and functionalities to interact effectively with AI tools.
- **Data Analysis:** Ability to interpret data outputs from AI systems to inform legal strategies.
- **Critical Thinking:** Evaluating AI-generated insights critically to ensure they align with legal standards and client interests.
- **Ethical Awareness:** Understanding the moral implications of AI use, including issues related to bias, transparency, and accountability.

6.3 Designing Effective Training Programs

Developing comprehensive training programs involves:

- **Needs Assessment:** Identify the specific AI tools to be implemented and the corresponding training requirements.
- **Customised Curriculum:** Develop training materials tailored to different roles within the firm, ensuring relevance and engagement.
- **Practical Workshops:** Incorporate hands-on sessions where legal professionals can use AI tools in simulated scenarios.
- **Continuous Learning:** Establish ongoing training opportunities to update staff on AI advancements and best practices.

6.4 Leveraging External Resources and Partnerships

To enhance training efforts, law firms can:

- **Collaborate with Educational Institutions:** Partner with universities or legal tech organisations to access specialised courses and certifications.
- **Engage with AI Vendors:** Utilize training programs offered by AI tool providers to gain insights into specific applications.
- **Participate in Professional Networks:** Join legal tech forums and associations to share knowledge and learn from industry peers.

By investing in targeted training and development, law firms can empower their professionals to effectively integrate AI into their practice, ensuring that technological advancements translate into improved legal services.

References:

- "AI Training for Lawyers: Bridging the Knowledge Gap," Legal Tech Munch, (legaltechmunch.com)
- "Essential Skills for AI Integration in Legal Practice," Tucan.ai, (tucan.ai)

- "Developing Effective AI Training Programs for Law Firms," Kelvin. Legal, (kelvin. legal)
- "Leveraging Partnerships for AI Training in Law Firms," Centerbase, (centre base.co

Adapting Law Firm Business Models in the Age of AI

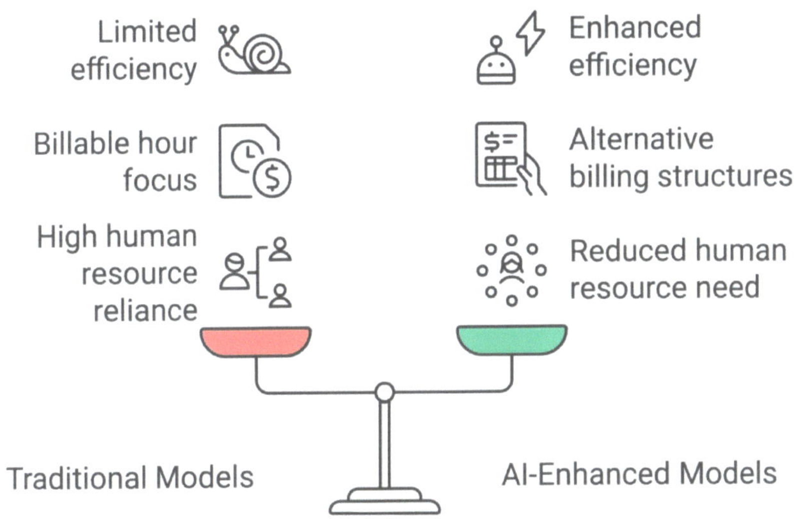

Adapting Law Firm Business Models in the Age of AI

7.1 Impact of AI on Traditional Legal Business Models

Artificial Intelligence (AI) integration is reshaping traditional legal business models, prompting law firms to reassess their operational strategies. AI automates routine tasks such as document review and legal research, enhancing efficiency and reducing the need for extensive human resources. This shift challenges the conventional billable hour model, as tasks that once required significant time can now be completed more swiftly. Consequently, firms are exploring alternative billing structures to align with the increased efficiency brought by AI.

Computerworld

7.2 Exploring Alternative Billing Structures

To adapt to the efficiencies introduced by AI, law firms are considering various billing models:

- **Flat-Fee Billing:** Charging a predetermined fee for specific services, providing clients with cost predictability and reflecting the reduced time investment due to AI efficiencies.
- **Value-Based Billing:** Pricing services based on the value delivered to the client rather than the time spent, emphasising outcomes and client satisfaction.
- **Subscription Models:** Offering clients ongoing access to legal services for a recurring fee, accommodating continuous support facilitated by AI tools.

These models align billing practices with AI integration's enhanced productivity and reduced timeframes.

7.3 Enhancing Client Services Through AI

AI enables law firms to offer more personalised and efficient services:

- **Predictive Analytics:** Utilizing AI to forecast case outcomes, assisting clients in making informed decisions.
- **Document Automation:** Streamlining the creation of legal documents, reducing turnaround times and minimising errors.
- **Virtual Assistants:** Implementing AI-driven chatbots to respond immediately to client inquiries, enhancing accessibility and responsiveness.

These advancements improve client satisfaction and position firms as technologically adept service providers.

7.4 Case Studies of Law Firms Successfully Adapting to AI

Case Study 1: Fennemore Craig

Fennemore Craig, a U.S. law firm, merged with technology-focused Lucent Law to integrate AI into their operations. This collaboration with OpenAI enhanced tasks such as drafting legal documents and improving pricing decisions, allowing the firm to offer alternative pricing options like flat fees. The integration aimed to boost efficiency, reduce unbillable hours, and increase revenue from alternative fee arrangements.

https://www.reuters.com/legal/legalindustry/law-firm-fennemore-touts-ai-fueled-fee-options-with-new-merger-2024-10-01/?utm_source=chatgpt.com

Case Study 2: Thomson Geer

Thomson Geer, an Australian law firm, invested in technological advancements and AI to modernise operations and expand market presence. Through its spin-off, TG Legal and Tech, the firm focused on high-volume services across various industries. The firm emphasised the importance of embracing tech-led disruption for future growth and now hires law graduates with additional qualifications in commerce or IT to integrate AI into their practice.

https://www.theaustralian.com.au/business/legal-affairs/thomson-geer-investing-in-tech-ai-to-keep-ahead-of-the-game/news-story/e54e3246fdb8de3f49a2c26adea14c02?utm_source=chatgpt.com

These examples demonstrate how law firms can adapt their business models to leverage AI, enhancing efficiency, client service, and profitability.

References:

- "GenAI surges in law firms: Will it spell the end of the billable hour?" Computerworld, (computerworld.com)
- "Will GenAI adoption end hourly billing in law firms?" Okoone, (okoone.com)
- "Law firm Fennemore touts AI-fueled fee options with a new merger," Reuters (reuters.com)
- "Thomson Geer taps into tech-led disruption," The Australian (theaustralian.com.au)

Navigating Ethical and Regulatory Challenges in AI Adoption

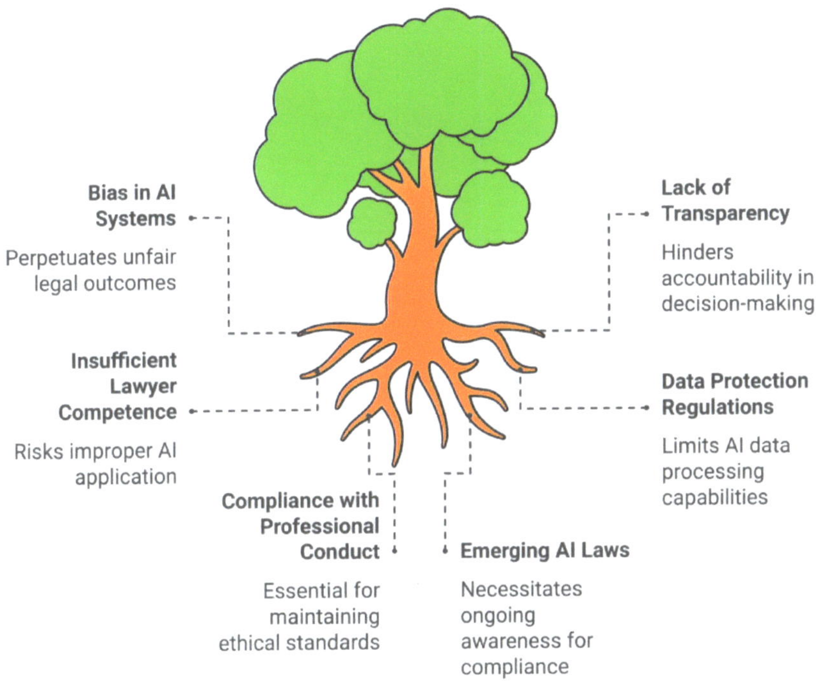

Navigating Ethical and Regulatory Challenges in AI Adoption

8.1 Understanding Ethical Considerations in AI Integration

Integrating Artificial Intelligence (AI) into legal practice introduces several ethical considerations that law firms must address to maintain professional integrity and client trust:

- **Bias and Fairness:** AI systems can inadvertently perpetuate existing biases in their training data, leading to unfair outcomes in legal contexts. For instance, if an AI tool is trained on historical legal decisions that contain biases, it may continue to reflect those biases in its analyses or recommendations.
- **Transparency and Accountability:** The "black box" nature of some AI algorithms makes it difficult to understand decisions, posing challenges for accountability and transparency in legal processes. This opacity can hinder a lawyer's ability to explain or justify AI-driven decisions to clients or courts.
- **Competence and Oversight:** Lawyers have an ethical duty to provide competent representation, including understanding their tools. Incorporating AI requires lawyers to attain sufficient knowledge to oversee AI applications effectively and ensure they are used appropriately.

8.2 Navigating Regulatory Frameworks Governing AI in Legal Practice

Law firms must navigate various regulatory frameworks that govern the use of AI in legal practice:

- **Data Protection Laws:** Regulations such as the General Data Protection Regulation (GDPR) in the European Union and the California Consumer Privacy Act (CCPA) in the United States impose strict requirements on data handling, impacting how AI systems process personal information.
- **Professional Conduct Rules:** Bar associations and legal regulatory bodies may have specific guidelines regarding the use of technology, including AI, in legal practice. Compliance with these rules is essential to uphold ethical standards.
- **Emerging AI Regulations:** Governments increasingly enact laws addressing AI usage, focusing on transparency, accountability, and bias mitigation. Staying informed about these developments is crucial for compliance.

8.3 Developing Internal Policies for Ethical AI Use

To ensure ethical AI integration, law firms should develop comprehensive internal policies:

- **Ethical Guidelines:** Establish protocols addressing ethical considerations, such as bias mitigation, transparency, and accountability in AI usage.
- **Data Privacy and Security Policies:** Implement measures to protect client confidentiality and comply with data protection regulations when using AI tools.
- **Usage Policies:** Define acceptable AI applications within the firm, specifying tasks suitable for AI assistance and those requiring human oversight.
- **Training and Competence:** To keep pace with technological advancements, provide ongoing education for staff on AI developments, ethical considerations, and best practices.

8.4 Case Studies of Ethical AI Implementation in Law Firms

Case Study 1: Implementing AI with Ethical Oversight

A mid-sized law firm integrated AI tools for document review and legal research. To address ethical concerns, the firm established an AI ethics committee responsible for overseeing AI applications, ensuring transparency, and mitigating biases. Regular audits were conducted to assess AI performance and adherence to ethical standards.

Case Study 2: Training Programs for Ethical AI Use

A large international law firm developed comprehensive training programs focusing on the ethical use of AI. These programs included workshops on identifying and mitigating biases, understanding AI decision-making processes, and maintaining client confidentiality. The firm also created a platform for employees to report ethical concerns about AI usage.

Law firms can integrate AI technologies responsibly by proactively addressing ethical and regulatory challenges, enhancing their practice while upholding professional standards and client trust.

References:

- "Legal Innovation and AI: Risks and Opportunities," American Bar Association,

  American Bar Association

- "Navigating the Legal Tech Landscape: Finding the Successful Path to Implementation in Law Firms," Jameson Legal,

  Jameson Legal

- "The Secrets To Success In Legal Tech Implementation," Above the Law,

  Above the Law

- "Implementing Legal AI In Law Firms," Lexitas,

  Lexitas

Addressing Privacy and Security Concerns in AI Adoption

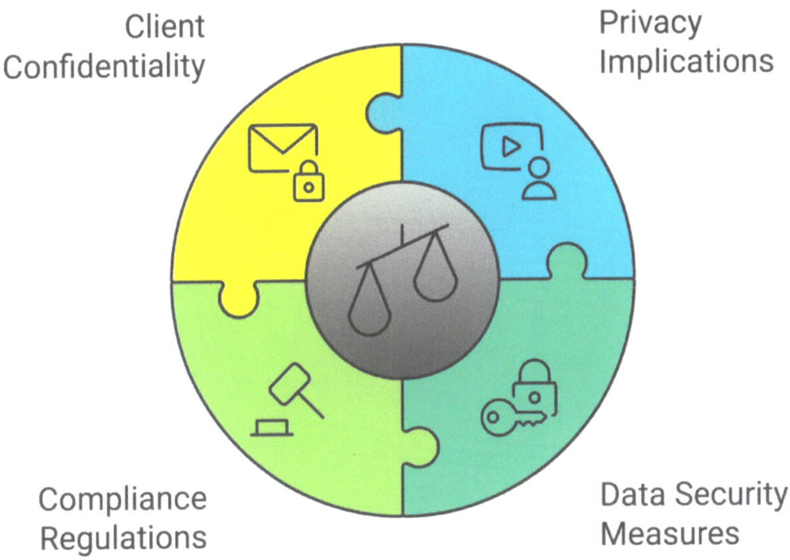

Addressing Privacy and Security Concerns in AI Adoption

9.1 Understanding Privacy Implications of AI in Legal Practice

Integrating Artificial Intelligence (AI) into legal practice necessitates a thorough understanding of privacy implications:

- **Data Collection and Processing:** AI systems often require substantial data inputs, including sensitive client information. Ensuring data collection and processing comply with privacy laws is paramount to maintaining client confidentiality.
- **Data Storage and Access:** Data used by AI tools must be stored securely, with strict access controls to prevent unauthorised access and potential breaches.
- **Data Sharing with Third Parties:** When AI solutions involve third-party vendors, it is crucial to assess their data handling practices to ensure they align with the firm's privacy standards.

9.2 Implementing Robust Data Security Measures

To safeguard data in AI applications, law firms should implement comprehensive security measures:

- **Encryption:** Utilize robust encryption protocols for data at rest and in transit to protect information from unauthorised access.
- **Access Controls:** Establish role-based access controls to ensure only authorised personnel can access sensitive data.

- **Regular Security Audits:** Conduct periodic assessments of AI systems and data storage solutions to identify and address vulnerabilities.
- **Incident Response Planning:** Develop and maintain a response plan for potential data breaches, including notification procedures and mitigation strategies.

9.3 Compliance with Data Protection Regulations

Law firms must ensure that their AI applications comply with relevant data protection laws:

- **General Data Protection Regulation (GDPR):** Adherence to GDPR is mandatory for firms operating in or serving clients from the European Union. The regulation emphasises data subject rights and stringent data handling practices.
- **California Consumer Privacy Act (CCPA):** U.S. firms dealing with California residents must comply with the CCPA, which grants consumers rights over their data and imposes obligations on businesses regarding data transparency and security.
- **Other Jurisdictional Laws:** Firms should stay informed about and comply with data protection laws applicable to their specific regions or clients.

9.4 Best Practices for Maintaining Client Confidentiality

To uphold client confidentiality in the context of AI adoption, law firms should:

- **Data Minimization:** Collect only the data necessary for specific AI applications to reduce exposure risks.

- **Anonymisation and Pseudonymization:** Where possible, anonymise or pseudonymise client data before processing it with AI tools to protect identities.
- **Vendor Due Diligence:** Thoroughly assess third-party AI vendors for their data security practices and compliance with privacy laws.
- **Employee Training:** Regularly train staff on data privacy principles, confidentiality, and the proper use of AI tools.

By proactively addressing privacy and security concerns, law firms can integrate AI technologies responsibly, ensuring the protection of client information and maintaining trust.

References:

- "Legal Innovation and AI: Risks and Opportunities," American Bar Association, (americanbar.org)
- "Navigating the Legal Tech Landscape: Finding the Successful Path to Implementation in Law Firms," Jameson Legal, (jamesonlegal.com)
- "The Secrets To Success In Legal Tech Implementation," Above the Law, (abovethelaw.com)
- "Implementing Legal AI In Law Firms," Lexitas, (lexitaslegal.com)

Evaluating and Selecting AI Vendors for Legal Practice

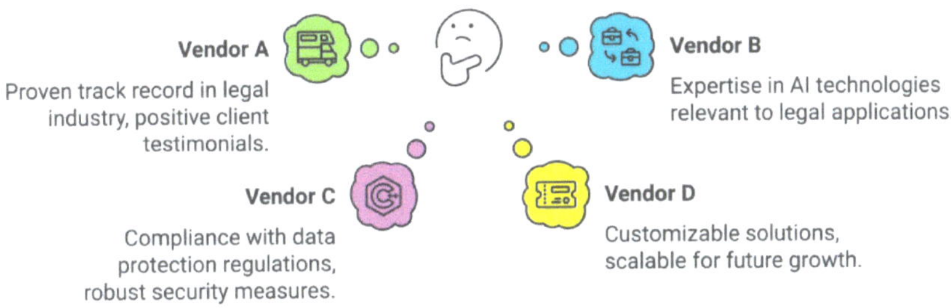

Evaluating and Selecting AI Vendors for Legal Practice

10.1 Establishing Evaluation Criteria for AI Vendors

Selecting the appropriate AI vendor is crucial for successful integration into legal practice. Law firms should consider the following criteria:

- **Reputation and Experience:** Assess the vendor's track record in the legal industry, including client testimonials and case studies demonstrating successful implementations.
- **Technical Expertise:** Evaluate the vendor's proficiency in AI technologies relevant to legal applications, such as natural language processing and machine learning.
- **Compliance and Security:** Ensure the vendor adheres to data protection regulations and implements robust security measures to safeguard sensitive information.
- **Customisation and Scalability:** Determine the vendor's ability to tailor solutions to the firm's needs and accommodate future growth.
- **Support and Training:** To facilitate smooth adoption and ongoing use, consider the availability of comprehensive support services and training programs.

10.2 Conducting Due Diligence on Potential Vendors

Thorough due diligence is essential to mitigate risks associated with vendor selection:

- **Financial Stability:** Review the vendor's economic health to ensure long-term viability and support.

- **Legal Compliance:** Verify that the vendor complies with relevant laws and industry standards, including data protection and privacy regulations.
- **References and Case Studies:** Request references from current clients and analyse case studies to gauge the vendor's performance and reliability.
- **Service Level Agreements (SLAs):** Examine SLAs to understand the vendor's commitments regarding uptime, response times, and issue resolution.

10.3 Negotiating Contracts and Service-Level Agreements

Effective negotiation of contracts and SLAs ensures clarity and protects the firm's interests:

- **Scope of Services:** Clearly define the services, including deliverables, timelines, and responsibilities.
- **Performance Metrics:** Establish measurable performance indicators to monitor the vendor's adherence to agreed-upon standards.
- **Data Ownership and Access:** Specify data ownership rights and ensure the firm retains access to its data, even if the partnership ends.
- **Confidentiality and Security:** Include clauses that mandate the vendor to maintain strict confidentiality and implement robust security measures.
- **Termination Clauses:** Define conditions under which the contract can be terminated and outline the data retrieval and service transition process.

10.4 Managing Vendor Relationships Post-Selection

Maintaining a productive relationship with the AI vendor post-selection is vital for ongoing success:

- **Regular Communication:** Establish consistent communication channels to address issues promptly and discuss potential improvements.
- **Performance Reviews:** Conduct periodic evaluations of the vendor's performance against SLAs and address deviations.
- **Feedback Mechanisms:** Implement systems for providing constructive feedback to the vendor, fostering continuous improvement.
- **Collaborative Planning:** Engage the vendor in strategic discussions about future needs and potential enhancements to the AI solution.

By meticulously evaluating and selecting AI vendors, law firms can ensure that their technological partners align with their strategic objectives, uphold ethical standards, and contribute to the firm's success.

References:

- "Legal Innovation and AI: Risks and Opportunities," American Bar Association, (americanbar.org)
- "Navigating the Legal Tech Landscape: Finding the Successful Path to Implementation in Law Firms," Jameson Legal, (jamesonlegal.com)
- "The Secrets To Success In Legal Tech Implementation," Above the Law, (abovethelaw.com)
- "Implementing Legal AI In Law Firms," Lexitas, (lexitaslegal.com)

Emerging Trends and Notable Startups in Legal AI

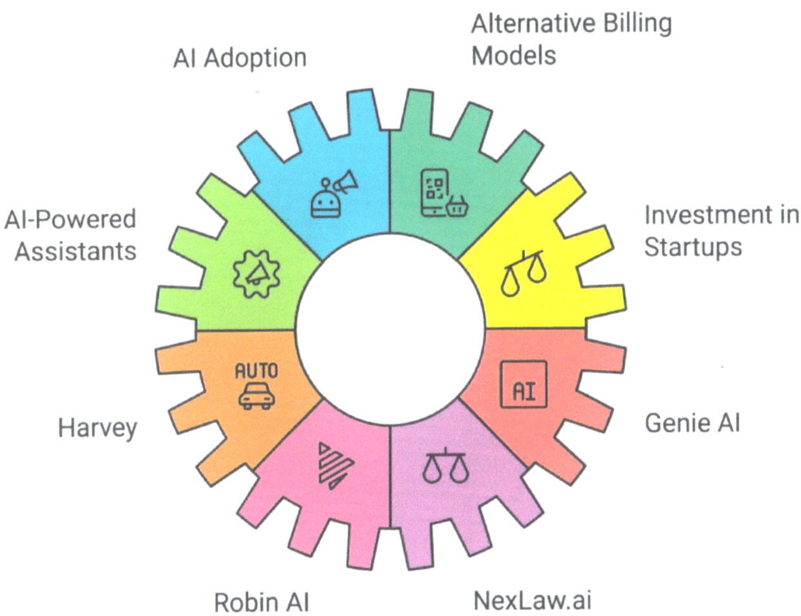

Emerging Trends and Notable Startups in Legal AI

The integration of Artificial Intelligence (AI) is transforming the legal industry. This chapter explores the latest trends and introduces prominent startups in charge of legal AI.

11. Current Trends in Legal AI

11.1 Accelerated AI Adoption in Law Firms

Law firms are increasingly integrating AI to enhance efficiency and reduce costs. A recent report indicates that AI adoption in law firms has surged from 19% to 79% within a year, prompting firms to realign their priorities and billing strategies.

11.2 Shift Towards Alternative Billing Models

Automating tasks like document review and legal research through AI challenges the traditional billable hour model. Firms are exploring flat fees or performance-based models to align with AI-driven efficiencies.

11.3 Emergence of AI-Powered Legal Assistants

AI-driven legal assistants are becoming prevalent, assisting lawyers with drafting documents, conducting research, managing contracts, streamlining workflows and improving accuracy.

11.4 Investment Surge in Legal Tech Startups

A significant increase in investments in legal tech startups focusing on AI solutions indicates strong confidence in AI's potential to revolutionise legal services.

Notable Legal AI Startups

Harvey

Harvey is an AI-powered "copilot" for lawyers. It offers tools for drafting documents, conducting legal research, and managing contracts. Backed by OpenAI, Harvey has raised $100 million to enhance its AI capabilities.

Genie AI

Genie AI is an editing platform that uses AI to draft and review legal documents. It offers personalised agreements across major global jurisdictions. The startup recently secured $17.8 million in funding led by Google Ventures.

Robin AI

Robin AI specialises in AI-powered contract management, featuring an AI copilot that can draft new contracts, review existing ones, and address queries efficiently. The company has experienced significant growth, with a 691% increase in search interest over five years.

NexLaw.ai

NexLaw.ai leverages advanced AI algorithms to streamline various aspects of legal work. It automates labour-intensive tasks and enables data-driven decision-making. The platform offers features designed to improve accuracy and efficiency in legal processes.

LawConnect

LawConnect is an AI-powered platform that provides free legal advice. It utilises AI to answer legal questions and connect users with lawyers for further assistance. The platform aims to democratise access to legal aid globally.

3. Implications for Legal Professionals

The rapid advancement of AI in the legal sector presents both opportunities and challenges:

- **Efficiency Gains:** AI can automate routine tasks, allowing legal professionals to focus on complex and strategic aspects of their work.
- **Ethical Considerations:** The use of AI necessitates careful attention to moral issues, including mitigation of bias, transparency, and client confidentiality.
- **Continuous Learning:** Legal professionals must stay informed about AI developments and acquire new skills to integrate AI tools into their practice effectively.

By embracing these trends and leveraging AI technologies, law firms can enhance their services, improve client satisfaction, and remain competitive in an evolving legal landscape.

Indian Legal AI Startups Transforming the Legal Landscape

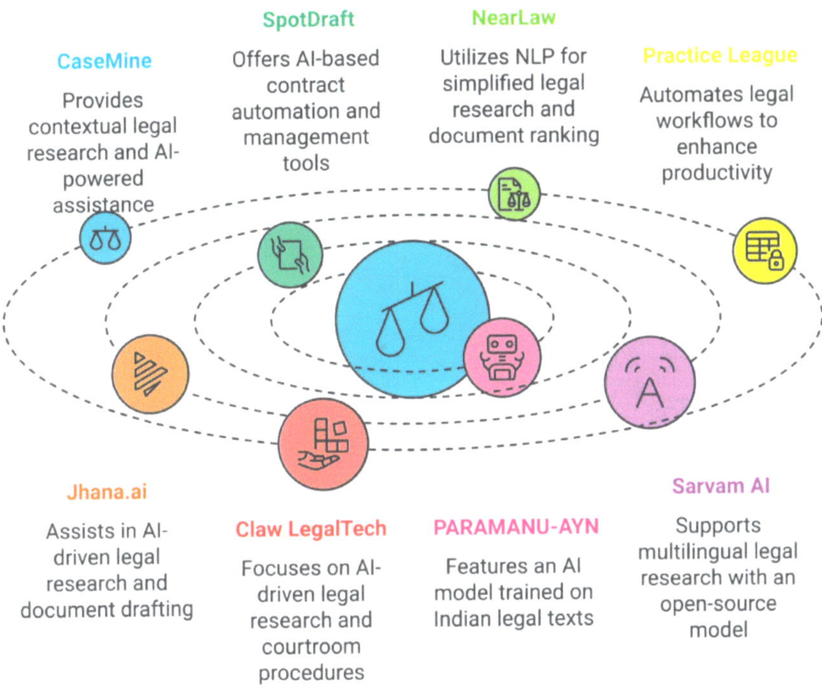

Indian Legal AI Startups Transforming the Legal Landscape

The Indian legal sector is undergoing a significant transformation due to artificial intelligence (AI) integration. Several innovative startups are at the forefront of this change, offering solutions that enhance efficiency, accuracy, and accessibility in legal services. This chapter highlights notable Indian legal AI startups and their contributions to the industry.

1. CaseMine

Overview: CaseMine, based in the National Capital Region (NCR), is a legal research and analysis platform founded by Aniruddha Yadav. The platform uses AI to provide contextual case law research, enabling lawyers to discover relevant precedents efficiently. In July 2023, CaseMine launched AMICUS, an AI-powered legal assistant with generative AI capabilities, marking a significant advancement in India's legal tech landscape.

Key Features:

- **Contextual Research:** Delivers case law research with contextual relevance, enhancing the quality of legal research.
- **AI-Powered Assistant:** AMICUS provides generative AI functionalities, assisting legal professionals with information retrieval and insights.

2. SpotDraft

Overview: Founded in 2017 by Shashank Bijapur, Madhav Bhagat, and Rohith Salim, SpotDraft offers an AI-based end-to-end legal technology solution. The platform enables organisations to review, draft, and manage contracts efficiently, streamlining the contract lifecycle.

Key Features:

- **Contract Automation:** Automates the drafting and review process, reducing time and minimising errors.
- **Management Tools:** Provides tools for tracking contract statuses and deadlines, ensuring compliance and organisation.

3. NearLaw

Overview: NearLaw, founded by Vikas Sahita, is a Mumbai-based AI startup offering solutions for lawyers, companies, and law firms. The platform utilises Natural Language Processing (NLP) technology to understand the relevance of case law, simplifying legal research.

Key Features:

- **CaseRanking:** Employs proprietary models to rank legal documents and judgments based on relevance.
- **Simplified Research:** Makes complex legal documents more accessible and understandable.

4. Practice League

Overview: Based in Pune, Practice League has transformed the workflow model of over 8,000 lawyers. The company offers SaaS-based products that automate legal practices, enhancing efficiency and productivity.

Key Features:

- **Workflow Automation:** Streamlines legal processes, reduces manual tasks, and improves accuracy.

- **Global Deployment:** Solutions are deployed in law firms across the globe, demonstrating scalability and adaptability.

5. Jhana.ai

Overview: Jhana.ai, a Bengaluru-based startup, offers an AI-powered legal research and drafting tool tailored to Indian legal practice. The platform aims to build an intelligent legal system and assist research and document preparation professionals.

Key Features:

- **AI-Driven Research:** Provides comprehensive legal research capabilities, enhancing the depth and breadth of information retrieval.
- **Drafting Assistance:** Assists in drafting legal documents, ensuring accuracy and adherence to legal standards.

6. Claw LegalTech

Overview: Claw LegalTech, founded in 2024 and based in New Delhi, focuses on revolutionising the legal industry with AI-driven solutions. Their products, including LegalGPT, AI Courtroom, and AI Drafter, streamline legal research, drafting, and courtroom procedures.

Key Features:

- **LegalGPT:** An AI tool for generating legal documents and content.
- **AI Courtroom:** Assists in managing courtroom procedures and documentation.
- **AI Drafter:** Automates the drafting of legal documents, enhancing efficiency.

7. PARAMANU-AYN by Gyan AI Research

Overview: Gyan AI Research introduced PARAMANU-AYN, an indigenously developed legal AI model trained exclusively on Indian legal documents, including Supreme Court cases, the Indian Constitution, and the Indian Penal Code.

Key Features:

- **Specialised Training:** Focused on Indian legal texts, providing contextually relevant insights.
- **Instruction-Tuned:** Trained on over 10,000 instructions covering various legal tasks, enhancing its applicability.

8. Sarvam AI

Overview: Sarvam AI, a Bengaluru-based startup, launched Sarvam 1, an open-source large language model tailored for Indian languages. The system supports 10 Indic languages, including Gujarati, Hindi, and Marathi, facilitating legal research and documentation in regional languages.

Key Features:

- **Multilingual Support:** Caters to a diverse linguistic demographic, promoting inclusivity.
- **Open-Source Model:** Encourages collaboration and continuous improvement within the legal tech community.

These startups exemplify the innovative spirit driving the transformation of India's legal landscape through AI. Addressing specific challenges within the legal sector contributes to a more efficient, accessible, and equitable legal system.

Top 25 AI Tools Revolutionizing Legal Practice

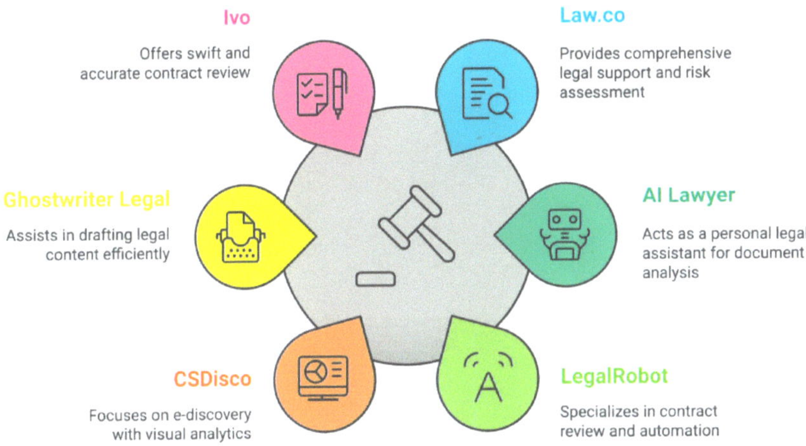

Top 25 AI Tools Revolutionizing Legal Practice

Artificial Intelligence (AI) is transforming the legal industry by automating routine tasks, enhancing research capabilities, and improving client services. Here are 25 notable AI tools that are aiding legal professionals:

1. **Law.co**: Offers comprehensive legal support, including access to extensive legal records, document review, and risk assessment.
2. **AI Lawyer**: Functions as a personal legal assistant, assisting with document analysis and providing personalized legal advice.
3. **LegalRobot**: Specializes in contract review and automation, featuring real-time risk assessment and legal brief writing assistance.
4. **CSDisco**: Focuses on e-discovery, offering rapid data processing and visual analytics for legal data sets.
5. **Ghostwriter Legal**: Assists in drafting legal content such as contracts, briefs, and memos, ensuring compliance and efficiency.
6. **Ivo**: An AI tool for swift and accurate contract review, highlighting key terms and assessing potential risks.
7. **BlueJ**: Provides predictive analytics for legal cases, offering plain-language insights based on extensive data analysis.
8. **Westlaw Edge**: A Thomson Reuters product that streamlines document review and other routine legal tasks.
9. **Briefpoint**: Automates the preparation of discovery requests and responses, streamlining the drafting process for various legal documents.

10. **Maigon**: An advanced AI tool for contract review, integrating deep learning technology for accuracy and efficiency.
11. **Legalese Decoder**: Simplifies complex legal documents by translating them into plain English, aiding in comprehension and client communication.
12. **Ferret.ai**: Provides exclusive relationship intelligence, helping lawyers avoid high-risk individuals and identify promising opportunities.
13. **Detangle.ai**: Offers AI-generated summaries of lengthy legal documents, highlighting important clauses and terms for better understanding.
14. **Casetext**: Features CoCounsel, an AI legal assistant that performs tasks like document review, legal research memos, and contract analysis.
15. **LinkSquares**: An AI-powered contract management tool that assists legal teams in drafting, reviewing, and executing agreements efficiently.
16. **Darrow AI**: Scans real-world data to detect harmful events, predict legislative outcomes, and assess the financial value of cases.
17. **Amto AI**: An AI legal assistant for drafting, providing suggestions on clauses, flagging risky language, and identifying revisions affecting other clauses.
18. **Paralegal AI**: Utilizes AI-powered legal research and summaries to help users find answers to legal questions efficiently.
19. **Harvey AI**: A generative AI tool that assists with contract analysis, due diligence, litigation, and regulatory compliance.
20. **Clio Duo**: An AI solution that automates routine tasks, prioritizes workflows, and enhances law practice efficiency.
21. **ChatGPT**: An AI-powered chatbot from OpenAI that assists in drafting legal documents, conducting research, and generating content.
22. **Lex Machina**: Provides legal analytics by reviewing and sorting court documents to discover trends with parties, lawyers, judges, and courts.

23. **DoNotPay**: An online legal service and chatbot that offers a "robot lawyer" service for contesting parking tickets and providing various other legal services.
24. **ContractMatrix**: A contract negotiation tool developed by Allen & Overy in collaboration with Microsoft and Harvey.
25. **Aalap**: An AI assistant for legal and paralegal functions in India, fine-tuned on instructions data related to specific Indian legal tasks.

These AI tools are revolutionizing legal practices by enhancing efficiency, accuracy, and client service.

Implementing AI in Legal Workflows: A Step-by-Step Guide for Law Firms

Implementing AI in Legal Workflows: A Step-by-Step Guide for Law Firms

1. Assess Current Workflows

- **Identify Routine Tasks**: Determine repetitive tasks suitable for automation, such as document review, contract analysis, and legal research.
- **Evaluate Pain Points**: Pinpoint areas where inefficiencies exist, leading to delays or increased costs.

2. Define Objectives

- **Set Clear Goals**: Establish specific objectives for AI integration, like reducing document review time by a certain percentage or improving research accuracy.
- **Align with Business Strategy**: Ensure AI initiatives support the firm's overall strategic goals and client service standards.

3. Research AI Solutions

- **Explore Available Tools**: Investigate AI tools tailored for legal applications, such as contract analysis platforms or legal research assistants.
- **Assess Compatibility**: Ensure potential AI solutions integrate seamlessly with existing systems and workflows.

4. Conduct a Pilot Program

- **Select a Test Area**: Choose a specific department or process to implement AI on a trial basis.

- **Monitor Performance**: Evaluate the AI tool's effectiveness in improving efficiency and accuracy during the pilot phase.

5. Train Staff

- **Provide Comprehensive Training**: Offer training sessions to familiarize staff with the new AI tools and their functionalities.
- **Encourage Adoption**: Address concerns and highlight the benefits to promote acceptance among team members.

6. Implement Gradually

- **Scale Implementation**: Based on pilot results, expand AI integration to other areas of the firm incrementally.
- **Monitor and Adjust**: Continuously assess performance and make necessary adjustments to optimize AI utilization.

7. Ensure Compliance and Ethics

- **Maintain Confidentiality**: Implement robust data security measures to protect client information.
- **Adhere to Ethical Standards**: Ensure AI usage complies with legal ethics and professional responsibility guidelines.

8. Evaluate and Optimize

- **Collect Feedback**: Gather input from staff and clients regarding the AI tools' effectiveness.
- **Refine Processes**: Use feedback to make improvements and enhance AI integration within the firm's operations.

By following these steps, legal firms can effectively incorporate AI into their workflows, leading to improved efficiency, accuracy, and client satisfaction.

www.ingramcontent.com/pod-product-compliance
Lightning Source LLC
LaVergne TN
LVHW051154210926
848486LV00005B/278